FM 999-4
Headquarters
Zombie Combat Command

Counter-Zombie Operations: Squad and Platoon

Table of Contents

    Page

Preface iii
Introduction..iv

CHAPTER 1 – CONCEPTS

    Most Basic Assumption...1-1
    Intelligence/Zombie 4 Report...1-1
    Vehicle Based Transport...1-2
    Resupply 1-2
    Available Troops...1-2
    The Zombie..1-2
    Zombie Fighting Equipment..1-4
    Tactics and Formations..1-6
    Phases 1-7
    Weather/Climate and Terrain 1-8
    Decontamination 1-11

CHAPTER 2 – PHASE 1

    General..2-1
    Phase 1 Objectives..2-1
    Combat Power...2-1
    Leader Skills..2-2
    Soldier Skills..2-2
    Platoon Operations During Phase 1...2-3
    Joining With Other Elements..2-5
    Transition To Phase 2..2-5
    Battle Drills...2-6
    Civilian Considerations 2-10
    Phase 1 Overview 2-10

Table of Contents Continued on Next Page

FM 999-4
Headquarters
Zombie Combat Command

CHAPTER 3 – PHASE 2

    General..3-1
    Phase 2 Objectives...3-1
    Combat Power..3-1
    Leader Skills...3-2
    Soldier Skills...3-2
    Platoon Operations During Phase 2..3-2
    Rescuing and Relieving..3-4
    Civilian Considerations...3-4
    Transition to Phase 3..3-6
    Regressing into Phase 1...3-6
    Battle Drills...3-6
    Phase 2 Overview...3-14

Chapter 4 – PHASE 3

    General...4-1
    Phase 3 Objectives...4-1
    Combat Power..4-1
    Leader Skills...4-2
    Soldier Skills...4-2
    Platoon Operations During Phase 3..4-3
    Civilian Considerations...4-4
    Transition to End of Counter-Zombie Operations..4-6
    Post-Zombie Combat Operations...4-6
    Battle Drills...4-6

APPENDIX

    A: Keeping Current with Zombie Combat Command A-1
    B: Additional Training Center B-1
    C: ZOCOM Online PX and Store...C-1
    D: Disclaimers D-1

DISTRIBUTION RESTRICTION: Approved for public release, distribution is limited.

FM 999-4

Preface

This manual provides doctrine, tactics, techniques and procedures on how all dismounted platoons and squads conduct close combat against Zombies in Counter-Zombie Operations (COZOP) within the United States. The United States Army has no doctrine regarding counter-Zombie operations beyond the borders of the United States at the time of print.

The term "Zombie" refers to a previously living biological organism which continues to move with purpose while showing no other sign of life (negative pulse, blood circulation, cognitive function etc).

This manual is the first of its kind and therefore supersedes no other manual. It is aligned with the Army's Counter-Zombie Warfare doctrine. It is not intended to be a stand-alone publication. Understanding of FM 999-3, Counter-Zombie Operations at the Fireteam Level and FM 999-5, Counter-Zombie Operations at the Company and Battalion Level, are essential.

In a Zombie infested environment, Zombies are not the only threat to achieving tactical, operational and strategic objectives. Understanding of other field manuals, notably FM 19-15 Civil Disturbances, FM 3-4 NBC Protection and FM 7-8 Infantry Rifle Platoon and Squad is highly recommended to achieve maximum effectiveness in a Zombie infested environment. Where there is conflicting information between FM 999-4 and other field manuals, information on FM 999-4 takes precedence in a Zombie infested environment.

The primary audiences for this manual are all United States Army personnel who may be tasked to lead a squad or platoon during the event of a Zombie outbreak which include, but are not limited to all first and second lieutenants, non-commissioned officers of all ranks and personnel holding the rank of specialist-4; instructors in TRADOC schools; and writers of Zombie warfare training literature. Secondary audiences include all other soldiers in the United States Army; and instructors and cadets at ROTC programs and military academies.

This manual is organized with separate chapters covering doctrine, nature of the Zombie disease, tactics, techniques, procedures and includes a tactical standing operating procedure. This manual is designed to fit in the hands of a motivated United States Army soldier. It should be used in the field as a guide to training and counter-Zombie operations. It is written with a heavy bias toward the tactics, techniques and procedures that make all soldiers successful in counter-Zombie operations. Leaders must be flexible to changing battlefield conditions but must not lose sight of the doctrinal principles outlined in Chapter 1, Doctrine. Additionally, all leaders should use this manual in developing an estimate of the situation and an analysis of mission, enemy, terrain, troops and time available and civilian considerations (METT-TC). This analysis ensures the formation of effective plans and successful mission execution.

For specific definitions for doctrine, tactics, techniques, procedures, drills and tactical SOP, refer to the preface of FM 7-8, Infantry Rifle Platoon and Squad.

Unless this publication states otherwise, masculine nouns or pronouns do not refer exclusively to men.

Electronic civilian distribution of this version of the manual is authorized through:

Army Zombie Combat School
http://zombiecombatcommand.com/

The proponent for this publication is the Zombie Combat School. Send comments and recommendations on DA Form 2028 (Recommended Changes to Publications and Blank Forms) directly to

Zombie Combat School
10710 Gateway N Blvd #222
El Paso, TX 79924

*See Appendix C for more information

FM 999-4
Introduction

Zombies are among the most dangerous hostiles in a combat environment. Zombies are known to have no fear, need no rest and have almost a sixth sense when it comes to detecting live mammals including humans. In order to prevent this threat from wiping out the human species, US forces must be continuously prepared to fight and win in Counter-Zombie Operations.

The fundamentals of Counter-Zombie Operations will read very much like a cross between infantry, military police and NBC defense roles and soldiers, especially leaders, need to know the fundamentals by heart.

This publication is organized in four parts. The first chapter focuses on information that is relevant to all phases of Counter-Zombie Operations and the following chapters each cover the three phases of Counter-Zombie Operations. The nature of the squad and platoon changes considerably depending on which phase of operations the US Army has entered. Leaders and commanders must also realize that not all areas of operations may be operating at the same phase level and different phases may be going on at the same time in the same area. Also, these phases do not necessarily occur in chronological order and for the most part, the first phase of Counter-Zombie Operations for most units will be Phase 2.

This manual focuses on the platoon and squad engaged in Counter-Zombie Operations but the soldier must realize that this is a small part of a much broader operation involving key phases.

These Phases are organized in order of the degree of control the force has over its area of operations. Brief descriptions of each phase are detailed in chapter 1.

Ultimately the goals of Counter-Zombie Operations are:

- Destroy all Zombies.
- Protect civilians.
- Protect/preserve infrastructure.

All Counter-Zombie Operations are to be executed according to METT-TC.

CHAPTER 1

CONCEPTS

The US Army's counter-Zombie doctrine is called Counter-Zombie Operations. It is based on time proven fundamentals, the experience of combat, and the forward thinking nature and imagination of the modern Army. The Counter-Zombie Operations doctrine provides guidance for all United States Army units and soldiers in the event of a Zombie outbreak.

Most Basic Assumptions

Because the United States Army has never engaged in combat against a Zombie threat, certain assumptions are made regarding the situation that most, if not all United States Army units and personnel will face during day one of the Zombie outbreak. These assumptions are based on the behaviors of both soldiers and the public during times of emergencies similar to that of a Zombie outbreak.

Intelligence

The soldier is most likely to receive his first notice of a Zombie outbreak through civilian news channels as the most likely source of a Zombie outbreak will be from within the civilian population. Eventually the best intelligence will come from within the military if civilian infrastructure and news networks are severely crippled during a Zombie outbreak. The transition from reliance on civilian information sources to military must be achieved quickly. All soldiers are to record all Zombie related observations report it to higher and/or S2:

Zombie 4 Report

Line 1: Date and Time (include year) of observation
Line 2: Unit making report
Line 3: Location of Unit (Specific grid coordinates preferred)
Line 4: Location of Zombies (Specific grid coordinates preferred)
Line 5: Number of Zombies
Line 6: Direction and Speed of Zombies
Line 7: Terrain Type
Line 8: Weather conditions
Line 9: Narrative
Line 10: Civilian numbers and condition
Line 11: Authentication

Fig 1.1 Initial information flow

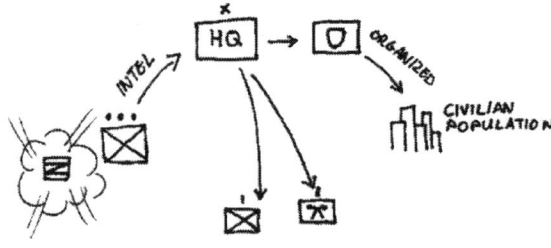

Fig 1.2 Desired information flow

Vehicle Based Transportation

Ground vehicle based transportation, especially in the first week of a large scale Zombie outbreak, is expected to be impossible. Roads are expected to be open only after engineers clear the roads of abandoned vehicles (Phase 2 through Phase 3). Until then, civilian traffic will clog all major and minor road ways. All mobility will be limited to foot, air or by vehicles capable of traversing unimproved terrain.

Resupply

Resupply will vary from phase to phase. A unit engaged in Phase 1 will find resupply extremely limited or impossible. Those in Phase 2 will find resupply favorable while those operating in Phase 3 will have extremely favorable resupply conditions.

Available Troops

Soldiers who commute, are on leave or are in Zombie affected areas (areas of infestation and areas affected by civilian panic) for any reason may not be able to report back to their respective units. All units are to understand and adapt to these developments. National Guard and Reserve units may be severely affected.

The Zombie

The Zombie is a formidable battlefield threat and is unlike most threats that the United States Army as an organization and the United States Army soldier as an individual physically, intellectually and psychologically trains to combat.

The Disease

The exact nature of the disease is unknown. It is not clear whether it is a virus or a germ. There are two different types of the disease that causes Zombification.

Type A Zombie Disease is airborne but is decidedly a weaker version of the disease. It does not cause death or any change in a live human being upon infection. Once the host (an infected person) dies, the disease takes over and the process of reanimation as a Zombie begins. The time period between death and reanimation is unclear and may be dependent upon certain variables such as the environment (humidity, temperature, elevation) and the level of exposure to the disease.

Type F Zombie Disease is fluid-borne and is much more potent. The Type F Zombie Disease causes symptoms such as fever, chills, headache, sweats, fatigue, nausea and vomiting typically within the hour from initial infection followed by death. The exact time between infection, death and reanimation depends on certain variables such as the individual's weight, immune system, health condition and environmental conditions such as temperature, humidity and elevation.

Zombie Stages, Identification and Action

The Zombie looks like a live human being in many ways but exhibits some key differences. Zombies can be identified with the following methods. Each method is organized in relation to infection stage.

- Stage 1, Infected: In this stage a healthy human being is infected with the disease. Type A Zombie Disease: there is no change and identification between an infected individual and an uninfected individual is impossible with the naked eye. Action: Only qualified medical personnel are authorized to tag a Type A infected soldier as "Type A Infected." Soldier is to resume regular duties. Civilians tagged as "Type A Infected" are to be quarantined.
Type F Zombie Disease: Individuals with a Type F infection can be identified with the naked eye. Before the individual exhibits fever, chills, headaches, sweats, fatigue, nausea and vomiting, the infected individual's pupils will not respond to light or darkness. Action: The infected individual must be killed immediately and the brain of the infected individual must be destroyed.
- Stage 2, Recently Reanimated Zombie: In this stage, the Zombie can look almost exactly like a live human being but with some differences. Its movement is slow and staggered, and its arms are extended forward. It may exhibit a groaning sound. Both Type A and Type F infections look identical from this stage forward. Action: Neutralize the Zombie by means of destroying its brain.
- Stage 3, Active Zombie: In this stage, the Zombie is most easily identified. Its skin is gray, shriveled and dry. It has almost no body fat. Its movement is more limited than a Recently Reanimated Zombie. Typically its clothing is either heavily damaged or missing. It may exhibit a groaning noise. Action: Neutralize the Zombie by means of destroying its brain.
- Stage 4, Neutralized Zombie: In this stage, the Zombie's brain has ceased to function and the Zombie exhibits no activity. It may look like a Stage 2 or Stage 3 Zombie or may be decomposed or damaged beyond recognition. Action: If security of the area is established by a battalion sized force or larger, the Neutralized Zombies are to be burned or cremated. In any other case, no action is to be taken against Neutralized Zombies. Large fires will attract Zombies to the source of the fire.

Zombie Fighting Equipment

In Counter-Zombie Operations, the soldier and his unit may be required to rely on weapons and equipment both in and outside of the US Army's arsenal. This section covers protective equipment and levels as well as weapons deemed effective and ineffective against Zombies.

Protective Equipment

The soldier is expected to wear any of the following types of uniforms as deemed appropriate by equipment availability and threat assessment:

Level 1: This level of protection shields the soldier from fluids with little sacrifice in combat capability. What is worn underneath the Gore Tex jacket and pants depends on the commander or leader's discretion in regards to weather.

- Helmet
- Eye protection
- Medical face mask or equivalent
- Rubber Gloves
- Gore Tex Jacket (with hood worn over the soldier's head under the helmet)
- Gore Tex Pants
- Combat Boots (With rubber boot covers if possible)

Level 2: This level of protection is to be assumed if the fluids excreted by Zombies proves to be highly toxic and infects through skin.

- Assume MOPP 4

Improvised Protection: If the unit does not have the necessary equipment to assume either Level 1 or 2 protection, improvised protection may be required. What is required is as follows: Protection from fluids and protection from ground debris (nails, broken glass etc) and head and face protection. Eyes, ears and mouths must be protected from fluids.

Weapons Effective Against Zombies

This section covers weapons that are effective against Zombies and how to employ the specific weapon.

Standard Weapons

- M-4/M-16 – The M-4 carbine or the M-16 are effective against Zombies and during Counter-Zombie Operations, it is the only personal firearm to be employed by soldiers when combating Zombies. Its accuracy is essential to performing head shots required to neutralize Zombies. The M-249 SAW is not to be employed due to ammunition considerations. The sheer number of Zombies present will put immense strain on ammunition supplies, so ammunition conservation is vital to force sustainment. The soldier must realize that rifle fire will attract Zombies.

- M6, M7 and M9 Bayonet – Bayonets are an ammunition conserving method of neutralizing Zombies. The bayonet must be attached to the M-4 or M-16. Grip method is slightly different. Although the back hand is on the neck of the rifle butt as in regular bayonet drills, the forehand must grip the magazine, and the rifle held sideways so that the magazine is parallel to the horizon. This is to ensure that the forearm does not get too close to the Zombie. Strong, fast thrusts to the head are required to penetrate the hard skull.

Non Standard Weapons

- Spear – Spears are highly recommended in counter-Zombie operations and are essential if the commander or leader intends to employ the phalanx (platoon and bigger only). The head of the spear must be able to penetrate a human skull and must be shaped in a way that would prevent the head from being lodged in the Zombie. Practical in open spaces only.
- Riot Shield – A riot shield or equivalent is required to employ the phalanx.
- Steel Pipe – A long, steel pipe can be used to crush skulls. Practical in open spaces only.
- Aluminum Baseball Bat – Baseball bats can be employed to crush skulls. This also represents the shortest melee weapon practical for use against Zombies.

Weapons Ineffective Against Zombies

This section covers weapons that are ineffective or impractical for use against Zombies.

Standard Weapons

- M-249 SAW – Conservation of ammunition is paramount in counter-Zombie operations and high fire volume will not psychologically suppress advancing Zombies.
- M-9 9mm Pistol – Doctrine demands headshots from distances beyond 50m to justify use of ammunition under regular circumstances.
- M-203 Grenade Launcher – Unless used to launch signal smoke, its additional weight will only fatigue the soldier for little benefit. A single 40mm grenade will neutralize only a handful of Zombies.

Non-Standard Weapons

- Crowbar – The shape of the crowbar causes it to lodge itself in the skull of the Zombie. To remove it would require the soldier to pull the Zombie's head towards himself. This exposes the soldier to a possible bite if the Zombie is not neutralized. Humans have survived gunshot wounds, heavy blows and impalement to the head. This will apply to Zombies as well.

- Chainsaw – Chainsaws are a waste of precious fuel and its noise attracts Zombies. It is also heavy, which will tax the endurance of the soldier.
- Pitchfork – The head of most pitchforks are not sturdy enough to penetrate skull.
- Flamethrower – Zombies do not fear pain nor death therefore, Zombies will advance into the fire. They will continue to advance until the heat destroys their brain. Zombie carcasses will set fire to the environment, which can endanger friendly forces and civilians.
- Axe – This weapon has a tendency to lodge itself in its target, posing a danger to the soldier employing it.
- Swords – Previously evaluated as an effective weapon against Zombies, upon further trials, they have proven to be ineffective due to lodging, damage and dullness that result from even moderate use.
- Crucifix and Garlic – Zombies are not affected by the presence of the Crucifix or garlic.
- Mallet and Stake – Zombies are not affected by stake penetration into the heart. Closing in to mallet and stake range for a skull penetration is extremely hazardous to the soldier.

Tactics and Formations

Tactics in Counter-Zombie Operations differ somewhat from conventional battlefield tactics. Counter-Zombie Operations have very limited use for weapons squads so they are referred to as the "fourth" squad in Counter-Zombie Operations tactics and formations.

There is also a fundamental difference in how the fireteam is organized. There is the Team Leader, a reloader and two riflemen in a fireteam during Counter-Zombie Operations. The reloader is typically the second most senior man in the fireteam and his primary role is to reload empty magazines for his teammates as well as assist the leader in land navigation and other tasks that require some experience. For specific information regarding the employment of fireteams in Counter-Zombie Operations, refer to FM 999-3, Counter-Zombie Operations at the Fireteam Level.

- **Arrow Head:** Basically a modified wedge formation, one squad takes point, two squads form the left and right flank, and the final fourth squad watches the rear. Ideal in most platoon sized movements and assaults, it provides a 360 degree field of view and fire. This is used in place of the platoon wedge formation.

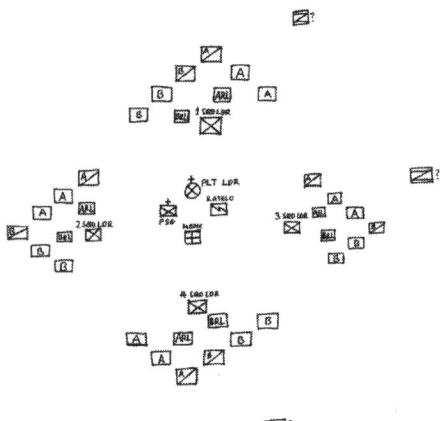

Fig 1.3 Arrow Head Formation

- **Line of Battle:** The platoon forms up two squads wide and two ranks deep. The first row can either be kneeling or in the prone, the second row standing or kneeling, depending on how the first row is deployed. This formation is best used in areas with a good field of fire and with Zombies coming from one direction. This is also the formation employed for Phalanxes.

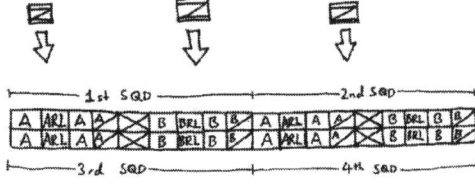

Fig 1.4 Line of battle/ Phalanx. [X] = squad leader. [A/] = Alpha Team Leader. [A] = a soldier in fireteam Alpha. [ARL] = Alpha Team Reloader.

Employment of the line and file formations are also practical in Counter-Zombie Operations, depending on the situation.

Phases

There are three phases in Counter-Zombie Operations and they do not necessarily occur in chronological order. Rather, they are ordered in the degree of control the force has over the situation. Phases can happen in tandem with one another. For example, on the east side of a metropolitan area, Counter-Zombie Operations may very well be at Phase 2 while on the west side of the same area, small and separated units might be struggling at Phase 1. Alternatively, city A might be enjoying a Phase 3 state while city B a hundred miles away might be in Phase 1 after a failed attempt by a large force to secure it.

Phase 1: In this phase, the force has the least amount of control over the situation. Small units, usually Company or smaller are completely cut off from the main force and focus on its own unit integrity. They have no practical means of resupply and/or communication with the main force and therefore do not engage in offensive operations against Zombies except for the purpose of linking with other units and only when it can be achieved quickly and with minimal losses. It is very possible for a squad or platoon to be in Phase 2 or Phase 3 of Counter-Zombie Operations and then find itself in Phase 1 a few hours later.

Fig 1.5 Typical Phase 1 scenario. A platoon is surrounded by tens of thousands of Zombies with no support.

Phase 2: In this phase, the force is in full control of itself but not the area of operations. This is typically the phase in which most squads and platoons will engage in Counter-Zombie Operations from the start. Working as a part of a much larger force with favorable support, squads and platoons will work to aggressively close in, engage and destroy Zombie formations and secure safe areas for uninfected civilians and civilians infected with the Type A Zombie disease while neutralizing Zombies.

Fig 1.6 Typical Phase 2 scenario. An infantry brigade assaults an urban area occupied by Zombies.

Phase 3: In this phase, the force is in full control of itself and the area of operations as well. Most dense population centers are safe of Zombies and major Zombie formations are destroyed. Squads and platoons in this phase work as small units and search for remaining Zombies and destroy them. Airmobile squads and platoons respond to reports of Zombies, using their superior mobility destroy any detected threats before they grow beyond control.

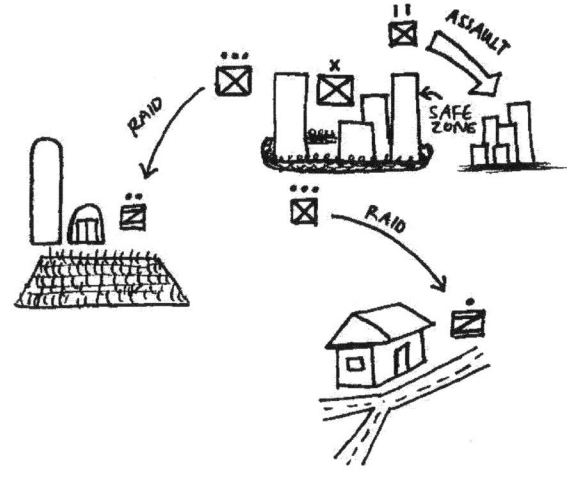

Fig 1.7 Typical Phase 3 scenario. A larger unit (in this case a brigade) sends out platoon sized QRFs to small outbreaks and sends a combat battalion to expand the safe zone.

Only the President of the United States has the authority to call an end to Counter-Zombie Operations.

Weather/Climate and Terrain

The effective employment of climate, weather and terrain can determine a platoon or squad's effectiveness against Zombies. The squad or platoon is much stronger against Zombies during daylight opposed to night time, so leaders must be mindful of BMNT and EENT.

Terrain:

This section covers which kinds of terrain squads and platoons have the advantage and disadvantage when engaging Zombies.

Advantageous Terrain:

Typically advantageous terrain will be one which offers elevation and a great line of sight. Zombies have trouble climbing slopes that are steeper than 45 degrees.

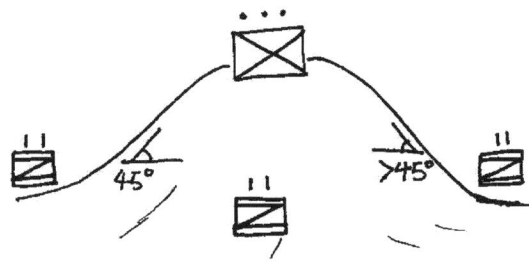

Fig 1.8 Platoon taking advantage of steep slope for protection.

When selecting advantageous terrain, leaders must consider:

- Adequately high elevation
- Restricted access
- Field of view/fire (minimum 50m)

Examples of terrain or geographic features that give platoons and squads the advantage are but not limited to:

- Rooftops or balconies of buildings if they are 3 stories high or higher.
- Tops of very steep desert mountains.
- Large, open fields (if operating as a part of a larger force or if Zombie numbers are adequately small).
- Overpasses, elevated walkways and other similar structures with access points destroyed or blocked off.

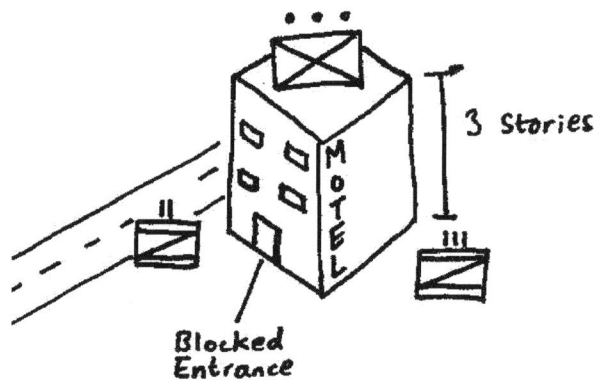

Fig 1.9 This building protects this platoon from thousands of hostile Zombies below.

Disadvantageous Terrain:

There are certain conditions where Zombies have the edge. Leaders must avoid these types of terrain and features unless required.

Disadvantageous terrain typically shares these characteristics:

- Low to no elevation
- Easy access
- Restricted field of view/fire (under 50m)

Examples of disadvantageous terrain are but not limited to:

- Dense forests.
- Jungles.
- Slums.
- Inside of buildings.
- Open fields (if force size is insufficient to the number of Zombies).
- Hilltops of gentle slopes.
- Most CQB situations.

Fig 1.10 This platoon is about to be wiped out.

Leaders must consider these factors when planning and executing missions during Counter-Zombie Operations.

Weather and Climate:

Weather and climate conditions affect the combat effectiveness of Zombies. Leaders must always be familiar with the effects weather and climate has on their own soldiers, but must also consider how they affect Zombies.

Weather/Climate Advantageous to Zombies:

Zombies are effective in weather that is comfortable for humans as well as hot weather. The temperature range in which Zombies are most effective are between 0 degrees Celsius and 50 degrees Celsius. Typically the Zombie is strong regardless of humidity.

Therefore Zombies are strongest in tropical conditions during the dry season where Zombies are at strength and the soldier is at a disadvantage due to heat and humidity.

Weather/Climate Disadvantageous to Zombies:

Winter is the biggest threat to Zombies as temperatures comfortably below freezing will stop a Zombie in his tracks. Unable to move, Zombies are most vulnerable during cold winters. The cold will not kill Zombies, however, as their bodies contain antifreeze which protect their cells from destruction from ice formation.

Rain can hinder Zombies somewhat in that unimproved surfaces, typically areas which have clay soil (like in the tropics), become extremely slippery when wet. It will affect the Zombie's ability to travel up slopes. However, in any other condition, rain will not affect the Zombie as much as it will affect the soldier.

Zombies are therefore weakest during the winter seasons when temperatures drop to around -15 degrees Celsius.

Decontamination

Many situations may require decontamination by the platoon or squad while operating in a Zombie-rich environment.

Chemical companies and teams will be fully engaged with decontamination operations and as a result, small decontamination work can and should be conducted by infantry platoons and squads.

Zombie Disease Presence

The Type A Zombie disease is airborne and there is nothing the platoon or squad can do to neutralize it. Considering that it has no effect on live humans, it can be ignored.

Type F Zombie diseases are fluid-borne and are a different story. Being extremely potent, they can infect, kill and reanimate a live human being if it enters the bloodstream of the live human being. Soldiers will be at risk to the Type F Zombie disease throughout Counter-Zombie Operations. The blood of Zombies will be cesspools of the Type F Zombie disease and must be decontaminated if possible.

Area Decontamination

Decontamination can be achieved by burning the infested area perfectly. It is not enough to simply expose the contaminated area or item to fire. However, in many situations, the use of perfect burning is impractical or impossible.

The best chemical to use for decontamination is Supertropical Bleach (STB). It can be applied as a dry powder or as slurry when mixed with water (always wear protective mask when preparing slurry).

If chemical weapons are being used against Zombies, STB will give off toxic vapors if the chemical agents are the G series of nerve agents (such as Sarin).

STB is also corrosive to metal.

STB should be in contact with the contaminated area for at least 30 minutes to be truly effective.

If STB is not available, household bleach may work.

Personnel Decontamination

Always decontaminate boots after exposure to a Zombie rich environment with a mixture of 2 parts STB and 3 parts sand. Always do this first.

Personal Equipment. After heavy exposure to a Zombie disease rich environment, soldiers must remove their protective clothing and deal with them accordingly:

- JSLIST: Remove, and wash thoroughly with warm, soapy water. Blast rinse with fresh water to remove soap and contaminants with physical force.

- MOPP: Remove and discard in designated bin for burning. Ensure bin is placed downwind from decontamination station. If replacement is not available, do not discard. Decontaminate with M295 decontamination kit or powdered bleach.
- ECWCS: Remove and wash thoroughly with warm, soapy water. Blast rinse with fresh water to remove soap and contaminants with physical force.
- Rain Coat: Remove and wash thoroughly with warm, soapy water. Blast rinse with fresh water to remove soap and contaminants with physical force.
- Gas Mask: Remove and remove filter canister. Wash thoroughly with warm, soapy water. Rinse thoroughly with fresh water.
- Eye protection: Remove and wash thoroughly in warm, soapy water and rinse thoroughly with fresh water.
- Disposable nose/face mask: Remove and discard in designated bin for burning.

Only dispose of items if replacements are available. If replacements are unavailable, leave as is.

Note that all decontamination here is not perfect. Only burning, which would render the equipment useless destroys the Zombie disease.

Personnel. The human body requires a thorough wash when possible after exposure to a Zombie disease rich environment.

Wash order must be as follows:

1) Thorough shower in cold water for at least 2 minutes.
2) Shower in warm water with generous amounts of soap. Much attention should be given to parts of the body where the skin folds (such as the inside of elbows and armpits). Minimum time is 5 minutes.
3) Rinse off in cold water for 3 minutes minimum. All the soap must be removed.
4) Dry with clean towel.

CHAPTER 2

Phase 1

General

In Phase 1, the squad and platoon must organize itself in the chaos that will inevitably ensue during Counter-Zombie Operations. Squad and platoon leaders must restore and maintain order and integrity of their respective elements and if possible, contact and rejoin its original unit or join with other elements. These include stragglers, separated fireteams and squads, other platoons and larger units.

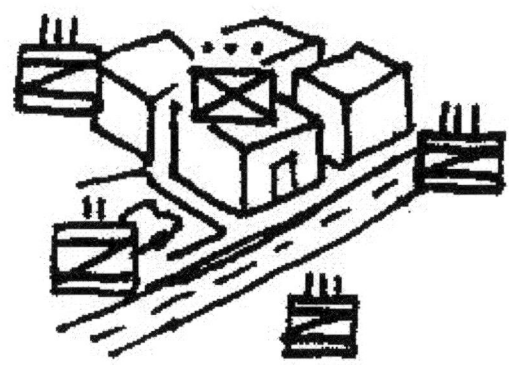

Fig 2.1 Typical Phase 1 Scenario

Phase 1 Objectives

The objectives of the squad and platoon in Phase 1 is as follows:

- Restore and maintain integrity of the squad and platoon.
- Enhance combat power by contacting and joining with other elements and units.
- Transition into Phase 2.

Both of these objectives need to be met in order to move from Phase 1 of operations to Phase 2.

Combat Power

Maneuver, firepower, protection and leadership make the four elements of combat power in Counter-Zombie Operations. The realities of operations during Phase 1 will affect these four elements.

Maneuver: Depending on the terrain and situation, the squad and platoon's ability to maneuver may vary from good to impossible. Platoons operating in sparsely populated areas with supporting transport vehicles may have exceptional maneuver capabilities whereas those operating in urban environments or areas within one hundred and fifty miles of urban or suburban areas may have extremely limited maneuver capabilities, even with the availability of ground transport vehicles. Within the first twenty-four hours of a major Zombie emergency, all major roads and highways are expected to be unusable due to heavy civilian traffic until cleared.

Firepower: During Phase 1, squads and platoons will be faced with a much reduced level of firepower than they are usually accustomed to. Cut off from larger elements, the only source of firepower will be organic.

Protection: In Phase 1, protection is the most important of the four elements of combat power. Because of the reduced level of firepower, the conservation of ammunition and other supplies is of the utmost importance. The squad and platoon must not engage in aggressive offensive operations as it may not be able to sustain itself beyond a few hours at most. If the squad or platoon's mobility is favorable, it must take the initiative and attempt to join with a larger element or combine with multiple small elements to create a larger one. If mobility is unfavorable, the squad or platoon must capture favorable defensive positions and hold out until relieved.

Leadership: In addition to the ability to coordinate the three elements of combat power, soldiers who have graduated from the Zombie Combat School would make favorable leaders during Counter-Zombie Operations.

Leader Skills

During Phase 1 of Counter-Zombie Operations, platoon and squad leaders must possess imagination and flexibility. They cannot rely on a book to solve problems and must not be influenced by the array of material from pop-culture. The United States Army soldier is a professional. Hollywood screenwriters are not. Nor can they lose the initiative by waiting to receive orders. Independent action is of the utmost importance during Phase 1. Skills acquired by attending and graduating from the Zombie Combat School will also further enhance a leader's ability to fight and win during Counter-Zombie Operations. Soldiers who have graduated from this school can be identified by their Zombie tab.

Fig 2.2 The Zombie skill tab

Soldier Skills

In addition to all the skills necessary to be a proficient war fighter, during Phase 1, the most important skill the individual soldier must possess is discipline. The soldier may be tempted to prematurely engage targets that may seem very soft at first without realizing the sheer mass of Zombies that are to follow. During Phase 1, the individual soldier is to exercise restraint in order to preserve combat power and is to engage only when his life is in immediate danger or under the direction of the squad or platoon leader.

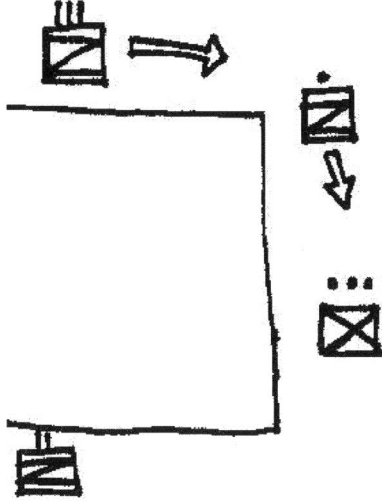

Fig 2.3 Soldiers may be tempted to engage a small group of Zombies, unaware of a large Zombie formation around the corner.

Platoon Operations during Phase 1

This section describes the three basic tactical operations undertaken by platoons and squads during Phase 1 of Counter-Zombie Operations – movement, offensive and defense.

Movement: Movement refers to the shifting of forces on the battlefield and may be the difference between establishing contact with a larger unit or being cut off. Effective movement can do two things:

- Increase combat power by joining with other units and soldiers, possibly to the point where transition to Phase 2 of Counter-Zombie Operations are viable.
- Gain access to more favorable defensive positions.

If movement is a realistic option, leaders should opt for the file formation to facilitate maximum speed. Movement is an option when these conditions are met:

- Movement and maneuver conditions are favorable.
- Immediate threat levels are low enough to allow for the employment of the file formation.
- The locations of friendly units or an even favorable defensive position are known.

If these conditions are not met, then a decision to move is highly questionable to move as:

- The unit will not be able to maintain or make distance from crowds or Zombies.
- There will be no meaningful place or direction to move towards.

Offense: Squads and platoons during Phase I of Counter-Zombie Operations do not engage in offensive operations unless it achieves any of the two goals:

- It enhances the squad or platoon's ability to move to and join with another element.
- It vastly enhances the squad or platoon's defensive position.

In either case, squads and platoons must engage offensively only if it can achieve its goals quickly and with minimum use of ammunition and supplies or if the alternative is to be destroyed. It is only used as a way to facilitate movement and only when absolutely necessary.

Fig 2.4 This platoon has decided to attack a small Zombie formation to take a good defensible position.

Defense: Due to the nature of Phase 1 operations, most of the squads and platoons will find themselves on the defensive. There are many characteristics of terrain and conditions that are favorable for defense.

- Elevation: The elevation should be high, preferably no lower than the second floor of a building and preferably higher than the third floor.
- Limited Access: The harder it is for Zombies to gain access, the better. These can include sheer cliffs, narrow and few staircases, ladders etc. Once the squad or platoon has occupied an area suitable for defense, it must seek to further reduce avenues of access by destroying them.
- Protection from the elements: Environmental elements such as excessive exposure to the sun, rain and other elements can and will reduce a squad or platoon's combat power. If the terrain allows, leaders should seek to defend areas that naturally provide some level of protection. For example, the top floor of a four story building might be a better place for the squad or platoon to occupy than the roof itself.
- Protection from civilians and other potential threats: Civilians may become extremely hostile during a Zombie outbreak and may seek to attack US Army units in order to gain access to supplies, weapons and/or to control terrain. A favorable defensive position, therefore, must also provide protection from small arms fire and violent crowds.

During Phase 1, a squad or platoon cannot hope to defend its ground primarily by firepower. A squad or platoon which chooses to do this will most likely perish.

Occupying a favorable elevated position is not the be-all and end-all of the art of defense for a squad or platoon engaged in Phase 1 of Counter-Zombie Operations. In addition to controlling a good defensive position, the squad or platoon must:

- Avoid detection: Light and noise discipline is paramount.

- Put itself first: The rescue of civilians is counter-productive. Supplies will be limited and some may have hostile intent.
- Avoid engagement: In heavily populated areas, there will most likely be more Zombies than the platoon has enough ammunition for. Also the sound of gunfire will attract more Zombies.
- Maintain situational awareness: The squad or platoon must have a 360 degree view of the area and be aware of developments.
- Collect intelligence: Record observations to pass to higher.

Joining With Other Elements

There are two general ways a squad or platoon in Phase 1 can join with other elements. These are by moving towards a friendly unit and *joining* or by being *rescued*. By definition, the unit(s) moving (or able to move) toward the other unit is joining, while a unit unable to move and is waiting for the other element's arrival is being rescued.

Joining and Rejoining

Squads or platoons which know the location of its own or other unit (by communication or other means) and have the means to reach them must do so. At the distance of 150m, a soldier from the squad or platoon must visually signal to the other unit about its intent by waving a highly visible object (such as a PT belt). This serves the purpose of ensuring that the waiting party does not mistake the squad or platoon attempting to join as a Zombie formation. The other unit must also signal back in a similar fashion. However, signaling by firing flares, blowing whistles and popping smoke are highly discouraged as that will attract Zombies and other hostiles.

Rescue

A squad or platoon unable to move will capture and control a favorable defensive position until it can be rescued. Radio and other forms of long range communication must be attempted but visual signals must also be used. These visual signs should not be visible from the ground and preferably only from the air. If possible, the visual signs must spell out the squad or platoon's unit designation (i.e. 1st Battalion 22nd Infantry Regiment, 4th Infantry Division should shape theirs as "1-22 4ID"). This is to make it possible to distinguish positions held by soldiers from those held by civilians.

Transition to Phase 2

The ultimate goal of any squad or platoon involved in Phase 1 of Counter-Zombie Operations is to transition into Phase 2, which is the first phase in which the fight is taken to the Zombies.

A series of conditions must be met before this is possible.

- There is a ready and reliable access to resupply and replacements.
- Reliable communication and contact is established with a unit Battalion size or larger.

Both of these conditions must be met before there is any hope of transitioning into Phase 2. If enough soldiers manage to regroup to form a Battalion sized element but do not have access to supplies, its combat power still remains insufficient to engage Zombies, secure safe areas and send out patrols to hunt and kill remaining Zombies in the area. Therefore, it is perfectly possible for Battalions possibly even undersized regiments to be unable to enter Phase 2 of Counter-Zombie Operations.

Battle Drills

These collections of drills exist to enable units to take action with minimal leader input and prevail during Phase 1 in a Zombie infested environment.

Battle Drill 1: Occupation of a building.

Situation: A platoon tasked with an objective in an urban environment becomes cut off from the main force and is surrounded on all sides by angry, panicked crowds and Zombies.

Step 1. Identify target and point of entry. The platoon leader identifies the target building and decides which point of entry to use.

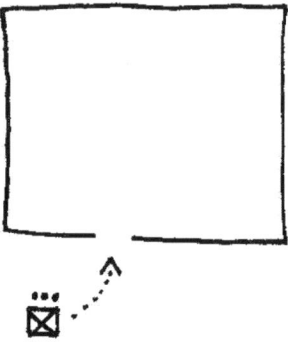

Fig 2.5 Platoon identifies and moves to selected entrance of selected building.

Step 2. Entry formation. One squad stacks on the door while three other squads provide security outwards in a semi circle.

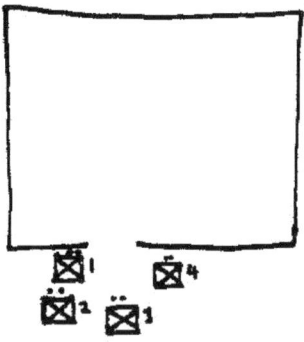

Fig 2.6 Entry formation. Squads 2, 3, and 4 are facing outwards.

Step 3. Entry and direction of clearing. The stacked 1st squad makes entry. 2nd squad follows. The stacked squad clears the left side of the first floor and the following squad secures the right side (relative to entry door and direction). As the two entry squads clear the rooms, they use the best of what is available (furniture) to block all other points of possible access (windows and doors).

Access points to block:

- Elevator doors
- Windows
    - If windows are too large, clear the room and block the doors leading to that room.
- Emergency exits to the building exterior.

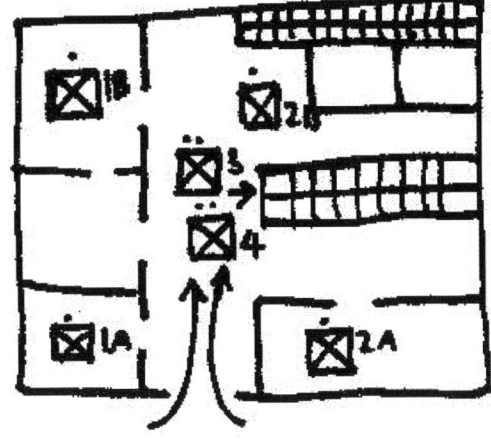

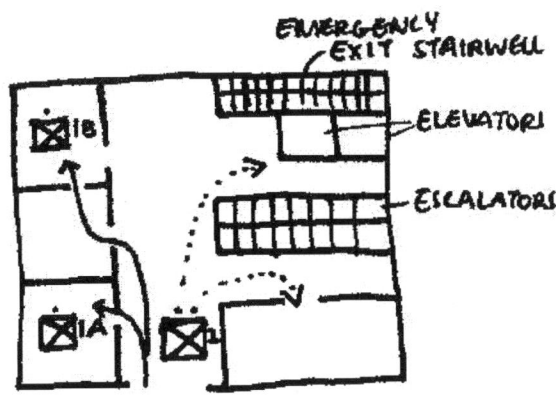

Fig 2.7 Clearing first floor.

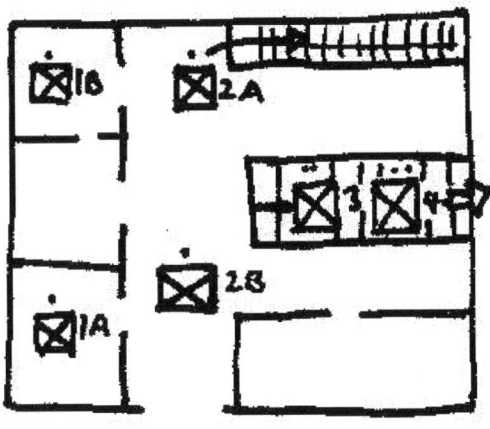

Fig 2.8 3rd and 4th squad movement.

Step 4a. Second floor. The two squads waiting outside enter and the platoon leader picks which stairwell to use. The two remaining squads (3 and 4) enter the second floor and clears it of Zombies in the same way squads 1 and 2 cleared the first floor. They must block the stairwells that the first and second squads are currently clearing (so that it can only be accessed through the first floor).

Step 4b. Additional stairwells. The first and second squads block the main entrance. The second squad leaves Fireteam Bravo, 2nd Squad to guard the first floor. Remaining fireteams split up and secure remaining stairwells to the second floor. The fireteams continue to clear the additional stairwells until they reach the top floor or the roof. The stairwell clearing teams of squads 1 and 2 stay in the stairwells if no additional stairwells exist. If additional stairwells exist, the fireteams are to wait until squads 3 and 4 clear the main parts of the building before going on to clear remaining stairwells.

Step 5. Securing all other floors. Squads 3 and 4 secure all additional floors until only the roof remains. When squads 1 and 2 are complete in securing all stairwells of Zombies, squads 3 and 4 access one stairwell and secure the roof.

Step 6. Establish position. The platoon is now ready to establish overwatch positions, establish contact with other units, and collect intelligence. Typically the four corners of the building will serve as guard posts manned by two to four soldiers at a time.

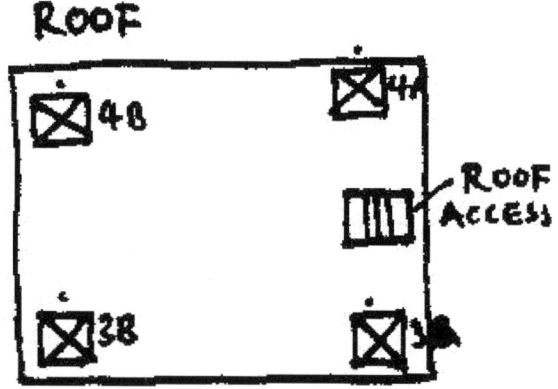

Fig 2.9 This provides a 360 degree field of view/fire over the surrounding area.

Overview:

Step 1: Identify building to occupy.

Step 2: Prepare for entry.

Step 3: Enter and secure first floor.

Step 4: Clear 2nd floor and stairs to 2nd floor.

Step 5: Secure all floors.

Step 6: Establish position.

Battle Drill 2: Occupation of a bridge.

Situation: A platoon tasked with an objective in an urban or rural environment near a bridge is cut off from the main force and is surrounded by angry crowds and Zombies.

Step 1 (a). Holding position (If Platoon is already on the bridge). The platoon is already on the bridge and the platoon leader realizes that they are physically cut off from the main force and are unable to move.

Step 1 (b). Fighting to the bridge (If platoon is not at the bridge). The platoon is cut off from the main force and the nearest and best structure for setting a defensive position is a bridge. The platoon leader selects the bridge as the new objective and using all his squads, attacks and fights his way to the nearest end of the bridge.

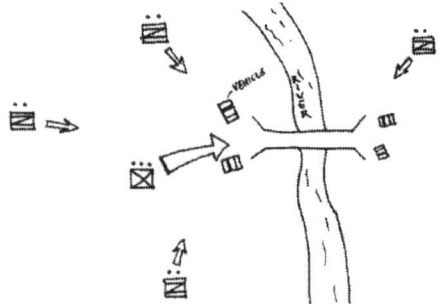

Fig 2.10 Fighting to the bridge.

Step 2. Blocking off one end of the bridge. Taking advantage of vehicles in the area, one end of the bridge is blocked off, preferably by means of using buses. Cars are tipped on their side to form barriers. Two squads are used for this duty while the other two provide security.

Step 3. Securing the bridge. Leaving one squad to improve the barrier and shoot any intruders, the other three squads move towards the other end of the bridge, clearing it of all threats.

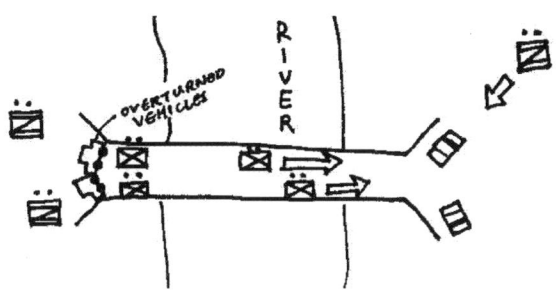

Fig 2.11 The west entrance of the bridge is blocked as two other squads work eastwards.

Step 4. Blocking off the other end of the bridge. After clearing the span of the bridge, the three squads arrive at the other end of it. It must be blocked off in the same manner as the first end that was blocked off. One squad creates a barrier while the other two squads provide security.

Step 5. Bridge secured. When both sides of the bridge are blocked, one of the squads which secured the second end of the bridge returns to the first end so that two squads hold each end of the bridge. Barriers must constantly be improved until no intruders can gain access. Other abandoned vehicles on the span of the bridge are to be used as

shelter. Intelligence must be collected so it can be passed onto higher at the soonest possible opportunity. Visual signals must be laid out as well as other attempts to re-establish contact with the main force and other elements.

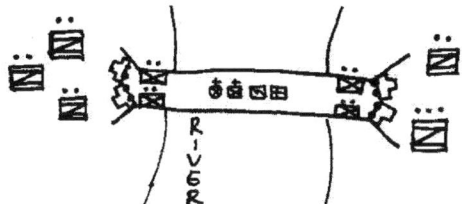

Fig 2.12 Secured bridge.

Overview:

Step 1: (a) Hold position on the bridge.
(b) Select bridge and move to it.

Step 2: Block off one end of the bridge.

Step 3: Clear span of bridge of hostiles.

Step 4: Block other end of bridge.

Step 5: Bridge secured.

Battle Drill 3: Breaking through to join or rejoin.

Situation(s): (a) The platoon is operating close to the main force but finds itself cut off by angry crowds and Zombies. The distance is short and the size of the crowd and Zombie formation, though manageable is becoming increasingly unmanageable. (b) The platoon has been holding a defensive position and a friendly element is now close enough to attempt to join or rejoin.

FM 999-4

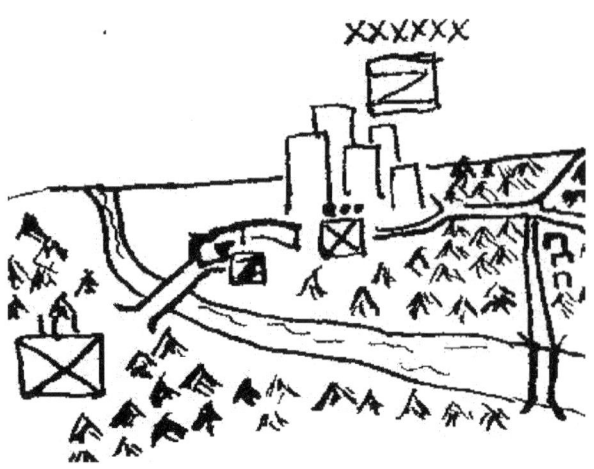

Fig 2.13 Infantry platoon avoids massive Zombie formation by attacking a Zombie formation a hundred strong to join with an infantry regiment.

Step 1. Direction of attack established. The platoon leader decides the best direction to attack and break through the hostile group or line.

Step 2. Attack formation established. The platoon assumes a line abreast formation to ensure maximum firepower.

Step 3. Attack commenced. The platoon will move towards its new objective by means of bounding overwatch.

Step 4: Join/Rejoin. Getting no closer than 100m to avoid blue-on-blue incidents, the platoon establishes 360 degree security and one fireteam is selected to signal the other element the platoon is about to join or rejoin.

Overview:

Step 1: Direction of attack established.

Step 2: Attack formation established.

Step 3: Attack.

Step 4: Join/Rejoin.

Civilian Considerations

The aiding of civilians in Phase 1 of Counter-Zombie Operations is discouraged as a platoon or squad is expected to quickly lose control of the situation if many civilians are involved. There will not be enough supplies to provide sustained aid to any civilians for any meaningful amount of time. All non-hostile civilians are to be ignored whereas hostile militias can be engaged in self defense. Civilian considerations are not a high priority in Phase 1 of Counter-Zombie Operations, unlike in Phases 2 and 3 where they are one of the key objectives.

Phase 1 Overview

Any unit that is unable to engage in sustained offensive operations due to lack of resources, communication or other reasons assumes that it has entered Phase 1 of Counter-Zombie Operations. The goal of every unit in Phase 1 of Counter-Zombie Operations is to transition into Phase 2. In this case, the platoon or squad may choose to either, occupy and secure defensible terrain or quickly move to rejoin with the force that it is supposed to be operating with, depending on which is achievable. Preserving or enhancing combat power is paramount in Phase 1 and the focus is on the platoon or squad and not on the larger picture of the area of operations.

CHAPTER 3

Phase 2

General

In Phase 2, the squad and platoon operate as a part of a much larger force with reliable access to resupply, replacements and communication. This is the typical phase in which active Army units will commence Counter-Zombie Operations. During Phase 2, the squad and platoon, in concert with other units, engages and destroys Zombie formations and maintains or gains control over key terrain such as urban areas, ports, bridges, and naturally defensible terrain. It also takes part in establishing quarantine areas and engages in bringing order to the civilian population. Once Phase 2 objectives are met, Counter-Zombie Operations transition into Phase 3.

Fig 3.1 A typical Phase 2 operation. A brigade is tasked with taking an urban area occupied by Zombies. The effort is fully supported by units operating out of their bases.

Phase 2 Objectives

The objectives of the squad and platoon in Phase 2 is as follows:

- Secure key terrain and infrastructure.
- Destroy Zombie formations.
- Control the civilian population.
- Establish quarantine areas.
- Transition into Phase 3.

Combat Power

Maneuver, firepower, protection and leadership make the four elements of combat power in Counter-Zombie Operations. Squads and platoons operating in Phase 2 of Counter-Zombie Operations will have excellent combat power.

Maneuver: Although roads are expected to be blocked for the most part, the availability of combat engineers and aviation assets will ensure favorable maneuver and movement options.

Firepower: Squads and platoons will not only be able to receive resupply for their own soldier carried weapons, is also able to call upon additional firepower such as artillery and air as necessary.

Protection: During Phase 2, protection is very favorable. In addition to the availability of armored vehicles, aviation assets allow squads and platoons to enter key areas of engagement via points which offer favorable protection features such as rooftops. Also, the availability of NBC assets help protect the squad and platoon from contamination.

Leadership: Reliable communications enable leaders to make more informed decisions based on his knowledge of the situation as it develops. As always, soldiers who have graduated from the Zombie Combat School would make favorable leaders during Counter-Zombie Operations.

Leader Skills

During Phase 2 of Counter-Zombie Operations, platoon and squad leaders must possess aggression, imagination and flexibility. They must be able to piece together what information they receive, along with the situation on the ground, and put it into context with the commander's intent and the orders that are relayed down to the leader. Situational awareness and aggression are of the utmost importance during Phase 2. The leader must have a good grasp of the situation immediately around him and in the area of operations as a whole. He must work in concert with elements operating in his vicinity and ensure that his squad or platoon stays relevant to the overall effort. The best way to do this is to ensure that his unit does not fall into Phase 1 of Counter-Zombie Operations.

Soldier Skills

The soldier must have all the proficiencies that make him an expert warfighter during Phase 2. He must possess excellent marksmanship, endurance and knowledge of his trade. Whether offensive operations occur in mountains, cities, plains or even beaches, the soldier must be able to perform and excel in his tasks. He must also be mentally tough as a Zombie infested American homeland is expected to be extremely stressful on the individual soldier, especially if he happens to be fighting in his home town.

Platoon Operations During Phase 2

This section describes the main tactical operations undertaken by platoons and squads during Phase 2 of Counter-Zombie Operations.

Maneuver: Maneuver refers to the shifting of forces on the battlefield in accordance with responding to or taking proactive action against Zombie formations. Effective maneuver can do a number of things:

- Allow the control of large areas with less manpower.
- Engage Zombies at a time and place that is most advantageous to the unit tasked with destroying them.
- Control and destroy Zombie outbreaks before they spiral out of control.
- Dictate the tempo and direction of battle.

During Phase 2, maneuver is key to controlling the area of operations. Every minute more Zombies are reanimated so time is of the essence.

Offense: Offense is the primary task of squads and platoons during Phase 2 of

Counter-Zombie Operations. They can engage in battle in one of two ways:

- As a part of a much larger force.
- As a squad or platoon operating independently.

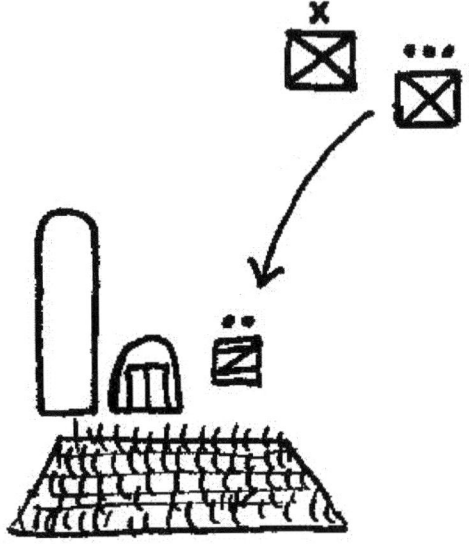

Fig 3.2 This platoon is operating as a part of a larger force.

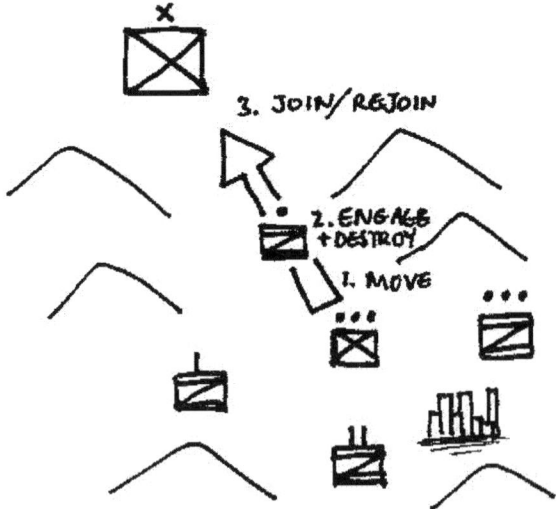

Fig 3.3 This platoon is operating independently but will soon be operating as a part of a larger force.

As a part of a much larger force, the squad or platoon will typically be involved in sweep and clear operations where very large formations roll in to an open countryside, town or city en masse to kill as many Zombies as possible in one sweep. When operating in a company or battalion sized formation, they may be tasked with taking and securing key terrain such as bridges, strategic buildings, and other areas of strategic or operational importance. When operating independently as a squad or platoon, they may be tasked to patrol secured areas or set up and observation posts.

Defense: Phase 2 is primarily an offensive phase of Counter-Zombie Operations but there are conditions where defense plays a key role. These include but are not limited to:

- Defending a key objective that has been taken in advance of the main force.
- Defending key facilities and installations (such as bases) which are static throughout the campaign.

The main difference in defense in Phase 2 as opposed to Phase 1 is that because of favorable resupply conditions, a platoon can conceivably defend its ground primarily by firepower.

Fig 3.4 This platoon is defending a key building, in this case, a civilian collection point. It is using both fires and terrain to protect civilians from a much larger force of Zombies.

Avoiding detection is not a high priority and in most cases, being visible is favorable. It boosts the morale of the civilian population and helps attract Zombies which makes destroying them easier.

When on the offensive, the bearing of flags and the playing of encouraging messages through the loudspeaker does wonders to the morale of the civilian population.

Rescuing and Relieving

Units engaged in Phase 2 of Counter-Zombie Operations are likely to run into a variety of groups needing rescue and relief. These include but are not limited to:

- Separated military units (These units are engaged in Phase 1 of Counter-Zombie Operations).
- Police units.
- Friendly militia groups.

During Phase 2, because of the lack of care facilities, the rescuing of the civilian population as a whole cannot be achieved. However, they can be given aid through food, water, and medicine. Providing relief to civilians during the offensive is paramount to winning the hearts and minds of the civilian population before more substantial support can be provided to them.

Military, police, and friendly militia groups which are rescued or relieved during the offensive are to be pulled back to rest, rearm, and be put into the replacement pool. They can expect to be put back into combat within twelve hours of relief.

Civilian Considerations

Protecting the civilian population as a whole is a primary objective of Counter-Zombie Operations. How many survive directly determines the speed in which the country can recover and resume normal life after the Zombie infestation is over. The leader must never forget that civilians, even well meaning ones, can pose a threat. Desperate crowds of civilians can overwhelm a squad or platoon that is unprepared to deal with them.

There are certain procedures when dealing with different classes of civilians.

Hostile civilians: Otherwise known as hostile militias or insurgents, the United States Army is expected to seek out, engage and destroy these elements. When a Zombie outbreak occurs, there will most likely be a power vacuum in major population centers and there are elements which want to fill that void. Along with Zombies, the squad and platoon will target and destroy these elements using conventional infantry tactics and must not hesitate to bring to bear the superior firepower of the military arsenal. Public Affairs and PSYOPS assets work to delegitimize and alienate these groups from the general population.

These hostile elements are expected to target food and medical supplies in particular to distribute to the public in order to win the hearts and minds of the public in their area of operations. Protection of convoys is paramount.

In addition to guerrilla warfare, they are expected to engage in civil disturbance operations as laid out in FM 3-19-15.

Disorderly civilians: These kinds of civilians are typical of those associated with civil disturbances in impromptu gatherings (FM 3-19-15, chap. 1). These civilians typically are reacting to the situation rather than creating it. They will typically gather around places that have some quantities of supplies they need such as food, water, clothing, firearms, and liquor. Typically they will engage in aggressive looting.

The squad or platoon, if operating as a part of a larger formation, will engage in dispersing these crowds with whatever means necessary then take control of the key places which are the target of such crowds. These include but are not limited to:

- Supermarkets.
- Pharmacies.

Once controlled, the supplies must be distributed in an orderly manner. This will achieve three things:

- Establish order in the area.
- Win the hearts and minds of the civilian populace.
- Provide aid to civilians, especially the children, the sick, and elderly who would otherwise not have access.

Stationary civilians: These civilians are people who have chosen to sit the outbreak out and are not on the move. They may or may not be armed with firearms. They are friendly and support the government and the military. Typically they will be running low on supplies. Squads and platoons which find these civilians during the course of Phase 2 must mark their locations and relay their information to higher so that help can be sent to them. Squads and platoons are not to deviate from their primary objective of destroying Zombie formations and establishing order in their area of operations.

Moving civilians: Often referred to as refugees, many civilians will choose to attempt to move away from the area of chaos. These civilians contribute to the chaos of the area of operations and limit mobility options on the ground by clogging roads and highways with vehicles. During Phase 2, the squad and platoon avoids these crowds if operating independently, and if operating as a part of a larger force, will force civilian traffic off roads so that engineers can clear the roads for military use. They may or may not be armed and are highly probable to turn angry and possibly even hostile once forced off the road. In order to ease tensions, aid will be provided to these civilians as soon as possible and the squad and platoon may take part in establishing camps and aid distribution centers, as well as providing security for quarantine facilities that will be established in areas of heavy civilian concentration.

Transition to Phase 3

The ultimate goal of Phase 2 of Counter-Zombie Operations is to transition into Phase 3. Once major population centers, key facilities and major roads are secure, quarantine areas established, and most Zombie formations are destroyed, Counter-Zombie Operations transitions into Phase 3.

Regressing into Phase 1

Units involved in Phase 2 of Counter-Zombie Operations constantly run the risk of regressing into Phase 1. That is, they fail to maintain contact with their higher echelon or become cut off and lose control of their battlespace. The squad and platoon must maintain a high level of situational awareness to avoid this.

Battle Drills

This collection of battle drills exist to allow squads and platoons to engage in aggressive offensive action against Zombies with minimal leader input.

Battle Drill 1: Street advance on foot (urban, light resistance).

Situation: Platoon is advancing down a road towards an objective. Zombie presence is sparse due to efforts of other friendly units in the area.

Step 1. Assume arrow head formation. Platoon forms an arrow head formation and gets ready to advance down the road towards the objective.

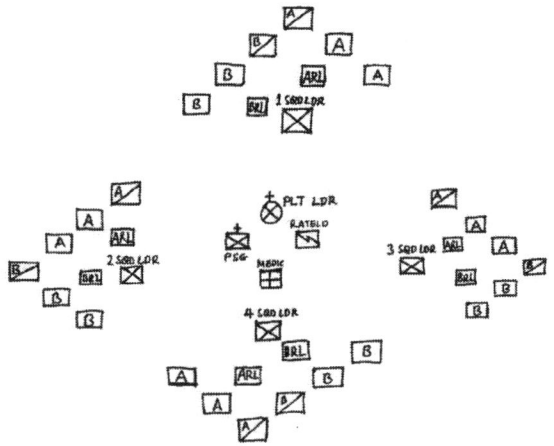

Fig 3.5 Arrow head formation.

Step 2. Set pace. Platoon advances no faster than a regular marching pace.

FM 999-4

Fig 3.6 A platoon advances down a wide road at a regular marching pace.

Fig 3.6a

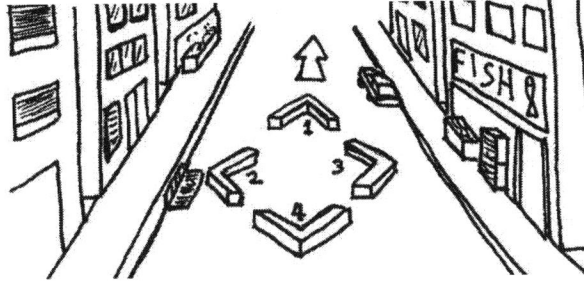

Fig 3.7 Shape of the squads while on the move.

Step 3. React to contact. Sporadic groups of Zombies, ranging in group sizes of five to fifty show up from different directions. Platoon halts when engaging Zombies to allow for maximum accuracy. Only headshots stop Zombies permanently. The squad engaged with the Zombie formation may form either a line or a line of battle formation (depending on space available) for maximum firepower. The other squads must hold their position.

Fig 3.8 The platoon makes contact to the front (12 o'clock).

Step 4. Resume movement/maneuver. Having neutralized immediate threats, the squad leader of the engaged squad signals to the platoon leader either by radio, visually or vocally that his squad is ready to move on.

Steps 3 and 4 may be repeated many times before the platoon reaches the objective.

Note: When engaging Zombies, the squad(s) engaged must do so with the maximum speed possible. Each soldier must know which Zombies are his to target immediately. This requires repetitive training at the squad level to a point where each member of the squad understands his target area of responsibility. Only when this teamwork is achieved is the squad, and the platoon as a result, truly effective in the arrow head formation. The speed in which Zombie formations can be dispatched can be the difference between life or death.

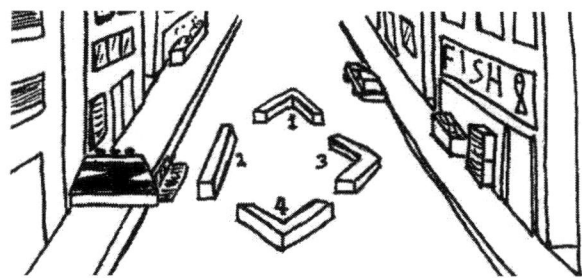

Fig 3.9 The platoon makes contact to the left (9 o'clock).

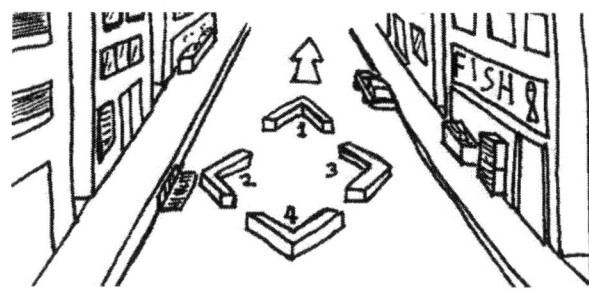

Fig 3.10 The platoon continues mission.

Overview:

Step 1: Assume arrow head formation.

Step 2: Move at an even pace.

Step 3: Stop to engage Zombies as necessary.

Step 4: Continue when threats are neutralized.

Battle Drill 2: Street advance on foot (urban, heavy resistance, unidirectional)

Situation: The platoon is operating in an urban environment and is advancing down a road towards its objective. Zombie resistance becomes very strong and further advance becomes impossible.

Step 1. Assume arrow head formation. Platoon assumes the arrow head formation and advances towards the objective.

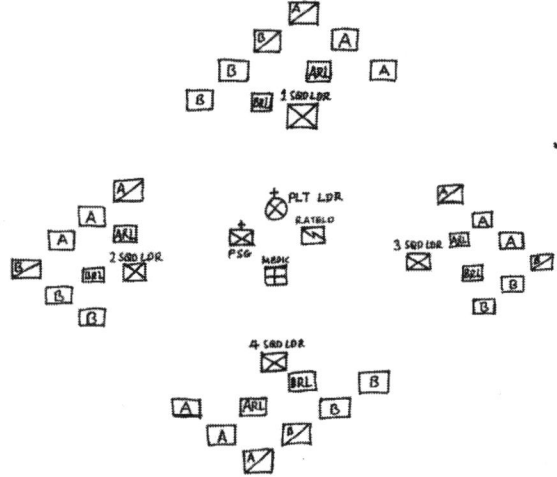

Fig 3.11 Arrow head formation.

Step 2. Set pace. The platoon advances no faster than a regular marching speed.

Step 3. React to contact. Platoon is encounters sporadic Zombie formations, ranging from five to fifty from a variety of directions. Platoon stops to engage each time. The squad or squads engaged assume a line or line of battle formation to ensure maximum firepower.

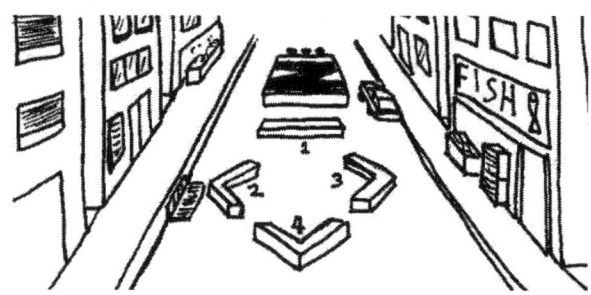

Fig 3.12 First squad assumes line formation for increased firepower.

Step 4. Increased Zombie presence. The sporadic appearance of small Zombie formations escalates into one where hundreds of Zombies move to attack the platoon from one direction. The platoon forms a line of battle, squads forming up with the squad furthest away from the direction of the new, larger Zombie formation.

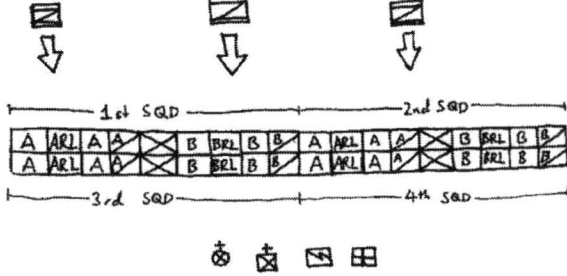

Fig 3.13 Line of battle. [X] denotes squad leader. [A/] denotes Alpha Team Leader. [A] Denotes a soldier in fireteam Alpha. [ARL] denotes Alpha Team Reloader.

Step 5. Engaging Zombie formation in platoon line of battle. The platoon engages the Zombie formation, using firepower to maintain a 50-100m distance between the platoon and the incoming Zombies. If possible, required, and practical, the platoon requests fire support.

Step 6. Resume movement/maneuver. When threats are neutralized, the platoon resumes its advance towards its objective. The platoon may choose a different route to avoid the mass of neutralized Zombies ahead. Direct exposure to the Type B Zombie disease with an open wound infects the individual immediately.

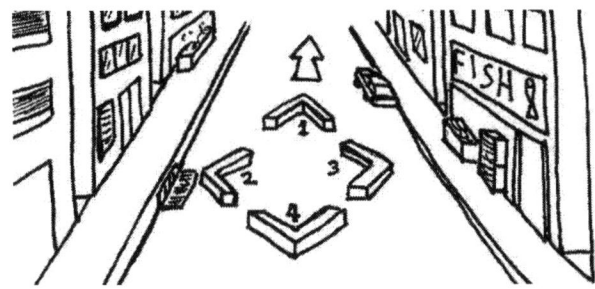

Fig 3.14 The platoon continues mission.

Overview:

Step 1: Assume arrow head formation.

Step 2: Maintain an even pace.

Step 3: Stop to engage small and sporadic Zombie formations.

Step 4: Change formation to line of battle when Zombie presence becomes very heavy.

Step 5: Engage from new formation. Maintain 50-100m distance between Zombies and platoon.

Step 6: Resume movement/maneuver.

Battle Drill 3: Building securing (vertical).

Situation: The platoon is operating in an urban environment and is tasked with securing a building (i.e. an office building or an apartment).

Step 1. Identify target and point of entry. The platoon leader identifies the target building and decides which point of entry to use.

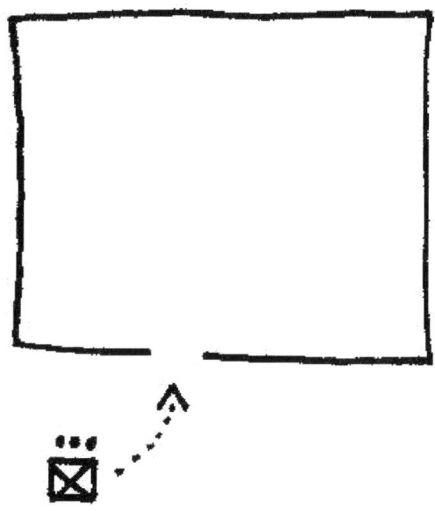

Fig 3.15 Platoon goes to target building and most viable point of entry.

Step 2. Entry formation. One squad stacks on the door while three other squads provide security outwards in a semi circle.

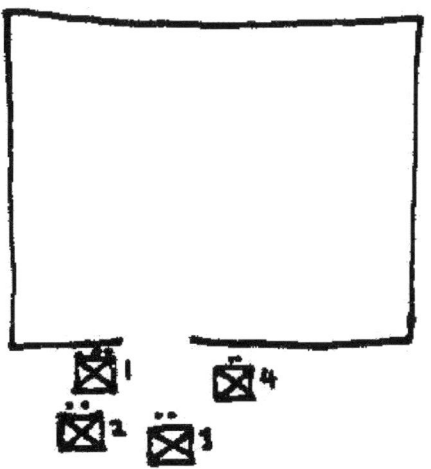

Fig 3.16 Platoon stacks up provides security on the entry point.

Step 3. Entry and direction of clearing. The stacked squad makes entry. Second squad follows. The stacked squad clears the left side of the first floor and the following squad secures the right side (relative to entry door and direction). As the two entry squads clear the rooms, they use the best of what is available (furniture) to block all other points of possible access (windows and doors).

Access points to block:

- Elevator doors
- Windows
    - If windows are too large, clear the room and block the doors leading to that room.
- Emergency exits to the building exterior.

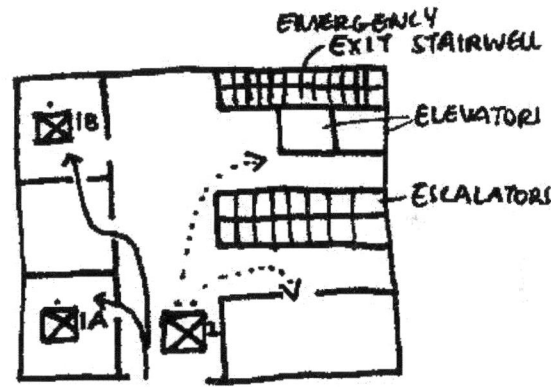

Fig 3.17 1st and 2nd squad clear the first floor

Step 4a. Second floor. The two squads waiting outside enter and the platoon leader picks which stairwell to use. The two remaining squads (3 and 4) enter the second floor and clears it of Zombies in the same way squads 1 and 2 cleared the first floor. They must block the stairwells that the first and second squads are currently clearing (so that it can only be accessed through the first floor).

Step 4b. Additional stairwells. The first and second squads block the main entrance. The second squad leaves Fireteam Bravo, 2nd Squad to guard the first floor. Remaining fireteams split up and secure remaining stairwells to the second floor. The fireteams continue to clear the additional stairwells until they reach the top floor or the roof. The stairwell clearing teams of squads 1 and 2 stay in the stairwells if no additional stairwells exist. If additional stairwells exist, the fireteams are to wait until squads 3 and 4 clear the main parts of the building before going on to clear remaining stairwells.

Step 5. Securing all other floors. Squads 3 and 4 secure all additional floors until only the roof remains. When squads 1 and 2 are complete in securing all stairwells of Zombies, squads 3 and 4 access one stairwell and secure the roof.

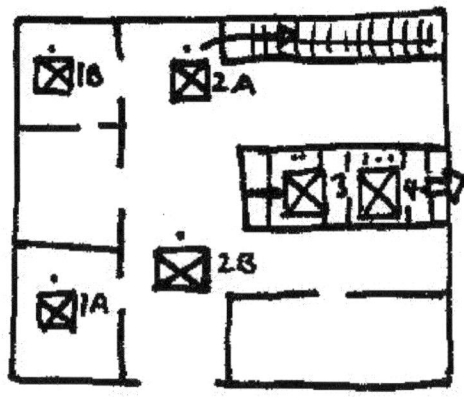

Fig 3.18 3rd and 4th squads move to the next floor while fireteam Alpha of 2nd squad clears emergency stairwell.

Step 6. Continuing mission. The platoon stays put if assigned to do so and exits the building if given further assignments. Upon exit, the platoon is to block the main entry door from the outside and mark "CLEARED MM/DD/YYYY," with visible spraypaint. "X" is to be marked on doors blocked from the inside. The platoon then carries on to its other objectives.

Fig 3.19 The platoon secures the building and occupies if the building is the objective.

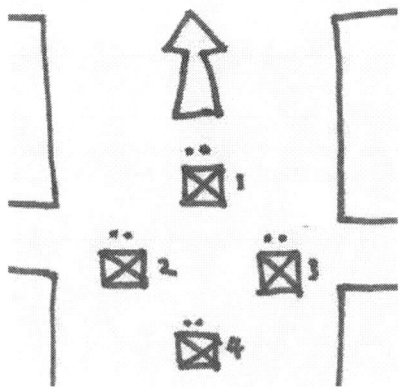

Fig 3.20 The platoon seals and labels the building and continues on to objective.

Overview:

Step 1: Identify building and point of entry.

Step 2: Prepare for entry.

Step 3: Enter and clear 1st floor.

- Squads 1 and 2.

Step 4a: Enter and clear 2nd floor.

- Squads 3 and 4.

Step 4b: Enter and clear additional stairwells.

- 1st squad and Fireteam Alpha of 2nd squad.
- Fireteam Bravo of 2nd squad guards 1st floor.

Step 5: Secure all additional floors.

Step 6: Hold or continue mission.

Battle Drill 4: Retreating Phalanx

Situation: Even in optimal conditions, the sheer number of Zombies makes ammunition conservation a top priority. The platoon here operates as a part of a much larger force, armed with shields and ten foot spears. The larger force is tasked with luring Zombies out of an urban area and into an open field where it can destroy the Zombie formation with minimal use of ammunition.

Step 1. Platoon assumes line of battle formation. The platoon forms up two ranks deep with its outer most soldiers shoulder to shoulder to that of the outer most soldier of the adjacent platoons. Soldiers in the front row hold shields, soldiers in the back row hold spears.

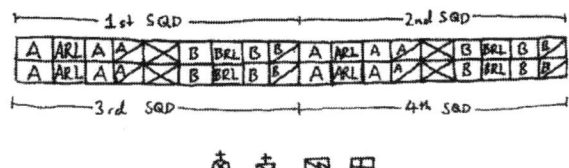

Fig 3.21 Line of battle formation.

Step 2. Platoon engages Zombies. When the Zombies reach the distance of about 8ft, the second row (armed with the spears) delivers a thrust to the head of the oncoming Zombies.

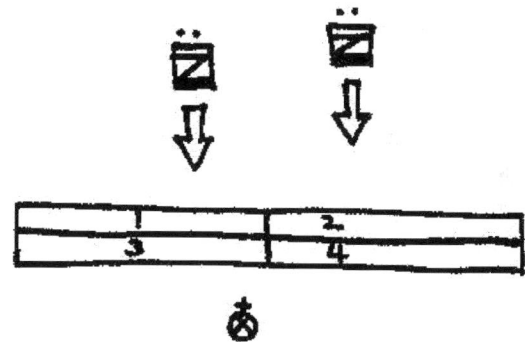

Fig 3.22 The platoon waits until Zombies are close enough to engage with spears in one thrust.

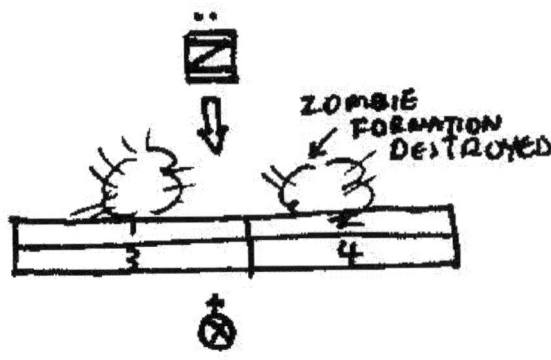

Fig 3.23 The platoon destroys the first line of Zombies.

Step 3. Platoon takes two steps back. To make more space, the platoon, in concert with the adjacent platoons, takes two steps back and repeats the process.

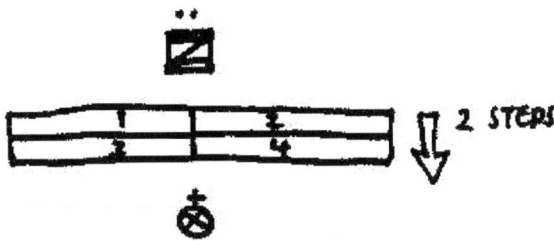

Fig 3.24 The platoon takes two steps back, ignoring the Zombie formation approaching it.

Note: The platoon must take a step back to protect itself from the Zombie disease that is in the "blood" of the fallen Zombies.

Step 4: Platoon opens fire. The platoon, as well as all adjacent units repeat steps 2 and 3 until they are at the run line, 50 meters from the firing line. This is predetermined by the senior commander in the field. From this point, the platoon runs back to the firing line, assumes a line of battle formation and engages remaining Zombies. All units will maintain a 50-100m kill distance between the oncoming Zombie formation and the platoon.

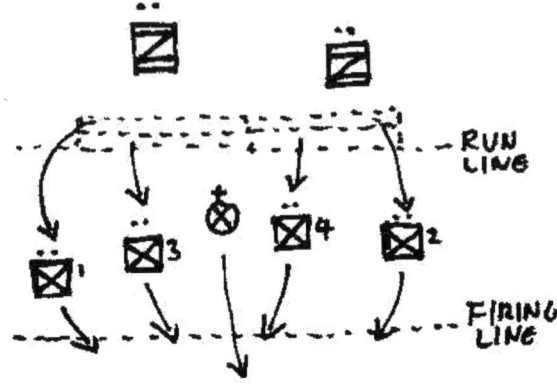

Fig 3.25 Running from the run line to the firing line.

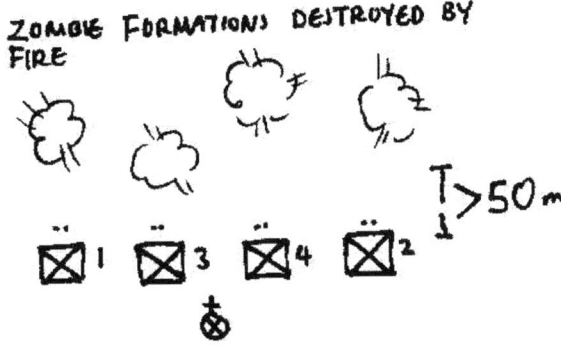

Fig 3.26 Zombies destroyed by fire from firing line.

Step 5. Hold formation. Even if the Zombie threat has been cleared in the immediate front of the platoon, other areas may still be engaged. The platoon is to hold formation to prevent flanking. The platoon holds formation until relieved.

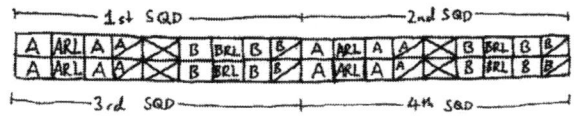

Fig 3.27 Line of battle formation.

Overview:

Step 1: Line of battle formation established.

Step 2: Zombies engaged with spears and shields.

Step 3: Two step retreat by platoon.

Step 4: Zombies engaged with firearms.

Step 5: Formation held until relieved.

Phase 2 Overview

Phase 2 is the primary offensive phase of Counter-Zombie Operations. Although the aiding and protecting of civilians is a priority, the destruction of Zombie formations is the highest priority. Taking full advantage of the platoon and squad's combat power to destroy Zombie formations and secure Zombie-free zones is the primary objective of Phase 2, and its successful completion naturally leads to a transition to Phase 3 of Counter-Zombie Operations.

CHAPTER 4

Phase 3

General

In Phase 3, major population centers have already been secured, as well as other key areas of strategic importance. For the most part, Zombie formations are not very common and life in the secured zones is beginning to have some sense of normality.

Squad and platoons operating in Phase 3 of Counter-Zombie Operations will find themselves taking part in many engagements as either, squads, platoons or companies. The vast majority of tasks will be to respond to Zombie sightings, especially outside of the secured zones as civilian law enforcement assets take over duties inside the secured zones.

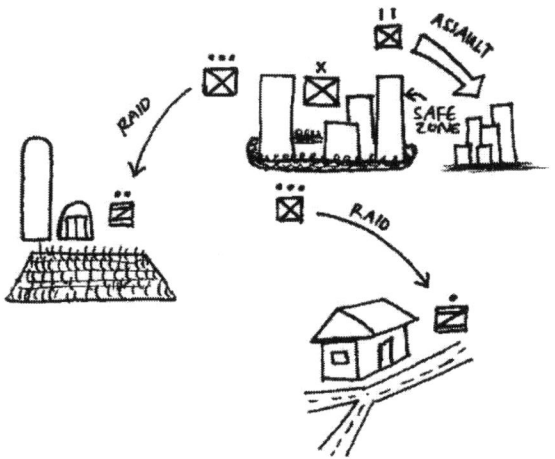

Fig 4.1 Typical Phase 3 scenario with platoon sized QRFs responding to outbreaks/sightings, platoon sized patrols, and battalion sized efforts in expanding the safe zones.

It is likely that Phase 3 can last several years after transitioning from Phase 2, and if not maintained with a state of vigilance, losing control of the situation and falling back into Phase 2 and for many, perhaps Phase 1 is a real possibility.

Phase 3 Objectives

The objectives of the squad and platoon in Phase 3 is as follows:

- Protect the surviving civilian population.
- Engage and destroy remaining Zombies.
- Ensure operation of key infrastructure.
- Gain the public's confidence in the military and the government's ability to control Zombie outbreaks.
- End Counter-Zombie Operations.

The first two objectives must be met in order to end Counter-Zombie Operations. Only the President of the United States has the authority to bring an end to Counter-Zombie Operations.

Combat Power

Maneuver, firepower, protection and leadership make the four elements of combat power. The conditions of Phase 3 of Counter-Zombie Operations will ensure that squads and platoons operating against Zombies will have more than enough combat power to tackle Zombie related threats.

Maneuver: Maneuver and movement options during Phase 3 will be very favorable. Almost all roads will be cleared of debris and air transport (fixed and rotary wing) will be back to normal. During the early months of Phase 3, traffic is expected to be even more favorable than during peacetime, as civilian traffic will be practically nonexistent outside of safe zones. If operable or operating oil drill sites, oil refineries and other petroleum manufacturing infrastructure is not secured and made to operate, movement options become limited over time.

Firepower: Overall, firepower will be at a very favorable state, with the securing of supply lines. If the manufacture of ammunition and explosives become an issue, firepower may become an issue as time goes on. However, commanders are expected to adapt to these situations and the appropriate use of ammunition can prevent critical shortages.

Protection: During Phase 3, squads and platoons will be operating in an environment where protection against Zombies and other threats is at an optimum. From NBC protection equipment, to riot shields, to favorable terrain (such as balconies of medium sized buildings), they will have the best protection against Zombies than during any other phase. Also there is the option of retreating behind well fortified defense positions in the event that a Zombie formation turns out to be larger than expected.

Leadership: During Phase 3, more and more soldiers will not only have the combat experience of fighting Zombies, but more leaders will graduate from Zombie combat schools. As a result, more squads and platoons tasked with engaging Zombies will be led by NCOs and officers trained in Counter-Zombie Operations.

Leader Skills

During Phase 3 of Counter-Zombie Operations, leaders must know much more than fighting Zombies. Troops who previously had no time to worry about home, friends, or other matters will start to find time to worry during the relative peace during Phase 3. Awareness of depression and possible potential suicide cases is a must, and leaders need to keep soldiers as busy as possible. During Phase 3, it is likely that soldiers will not be discharged from service and those with expiring or expired contracts will be stop-lossed.

Access to psychiatric, religious and other points of assistance will be available during Phase 3, and leaders must know to use these assets to maintain morale, order, and discipline within the ranks.

Leaders must also be proficient in troop leading skills and respond to, engage, and destroy Zombies as assigned.

Soldier Skills

Psychologically, Phase 3 may be the most stressful for the individual soldier because he will have the time to remember, reflect and think about the events that had unfolded during the Zombie outbreak. Soldiers must be able to accept and adapt to the new realities, not only within the Army but also in society as a whole. Soldiers must assist each other in stress management and be on the lookout for other soldiers who may not be adapting well to the new realities. Seeking professional help must be encouraged and every effort must be made from within the ranks to not stigmatize soldiers who seek help. Seeking help is professional; waiting until it is too late is not.

Soldiers must keep busy. If daily tasks and routine is insufficient, the soldier must find a hobby to keep his mind occupied.

In addition to responding to and coping with a changed social environment, soldiers must still maintain a state of vigilance and hone their warfighting skills. The soldier must be able to perform his combat duties as assigned.

Platoon Operations during Phase 3

This section describes three basic tactical operations undertaken by platoons and squads during Phase 3 of Counter-Zombie Operations.

Movement: Movement refers to the shifting of forces on the battlefield and must be performed with speed and precision to respond to and eradicate Zombie formations and outbreaks as they are observed. Speed and accuracy of movement is paramount in order to:

- Control further Zombie outbreaks.
- Gain public confidence in that the military is in control of the Zombie threat.

Commanders must ensure that movement conditions are favorable by ensuring that their unit leaders have fast and easy access to ground and air transportation assets and roads are light on civilian traffic. They must also assign subordinate units with Quick Reaction Force duties on rotation on a 24 hour, 7 days a week basis.

Quick Reaction Force: When a unit (typically a platoon), is tasked as a Quick Reaction Force, the leader is to ensure maximum vigilance. The time from the platoon receiving its orders to the time the platoon is on the transport vehicle (truck, APC, helicopter etc.) should be no more than 15 minutes.

If speed is deemed a higher priority than size per the nature of the Zombie threat in the area, commanders and leaders may choose to opt for faster and lighter squad sized QRFs. These must be able to respond to a "go" order in less than 5 minutes.

The ability to respond to reports of Zombies quickly and accurately is paramount in Phase 3 of Counter-Zombie Operations.

Offense: During Phase 3 of Counter-Zombie Operations, quick, accurate, and aggressive attacks on Zombies is the best way to end Counter-Zombie Operations. There are two main offensive efforts during Phase 3:

- Reaction: These are operations where the squad or platoon reacts to an action initiated by Zombies. For example, a QRF responding to a Zombie sighting.

- Patrol/Reconnaissance: These are operations where the squad or platoon seeks to find Zombies outside of the safe zones.

Defense: Protecting the civilian population that has been saved during Phase 2 of Counter-Zombie Operations is one of the primary goals of Phase 3 and Counter-Zombie Operations as a whole. Platoons and squads assigned to safe zone security duty must be vigilant at all times. The scent given by live humans attracts Zombies, so an area habited by tens of thousands of people will be a target for surviving Zombies. It is not a matter of if, rather when Zombies will appear around the perimeter.

No Zombie should ever be allowed to get within 50m of the perimeter wall.

A big threat to safe zone perimeter security is not from outside elements, rather, it is from within the mind of the soldier. With routine and long periods of time to remember and reflect, depression and possibly even suicide incidents are expected to increase. The worst would be fratricide. When assigned to defensive duties, officers and NCOs must work just as hard, if not harder to deal with these internal threats as with external threats.

Civilian Considerations

As with Phase 2, protecting the civilian population as a whole is a primary objective of Counter-Zombie Operations. Unlike Phase 2, however, in Phase 3, much of the civilian populace is residing within safe zones. Working with the civilian populace during Phase 3 is much more complicated than during any other phase. There are two major categories to which other subcategories of civilians belong to in this phase, Civilians in Safe Zones and Civilians Outside Safe Zones.

Civilians in Safe Zones:

These populations reside within safe zones and live within them by their own free will.

Hostile civilians: Due to the rationing of supplies such as food, medicine and luxuries, especially during the early months and perhaps years of Phase 3, a minority of civilians within the safe zones are expected to become hostile. These insurgents must be dealt with swiftly and with little fanfare. As for combating insurgency movements as a whole, refer to FM 3-24 Counterinsurgency, FM 3-24.2 Tactics in Counterinsurgency and FM 3-07 Stability Operations. Eventually civilian law enforcement agencies will take over internal security within safe areas and internal issues including insurgencies will be dealt with by law enforcement.

Disorderly civilians: These civilians are typically those associated with civil disturbances in impromptu gatherings as explained in FM 3-19-15. Riots and demonstrations may occur during supply distribution at distribution locations. Lethal force is not authorized on demonstrators and rioters unless demonstrators or rioters engage soldiers with lethal force and intent. Police units (military and/or civilian) will be assisted by other Army units in controlling disorderly crowds. Infantry platoons and squads will be trained in crowd control as Phase 3 comes into effect.

Orderly civilians: The rest of the populace within the safe zones fall into this category. Soldiers are to maintain excellent relations with these civilians and must conduct themselves with the highest level of courtesy and integrity. Some simple actions that can go a long way include:

- Helping old women cross the road.
- Helping retrieve a cat from a tree.
- Smiling.

Simple acts of kindness on a regular basis can prevent the growth of insurgency movements.

Civilians Outside Safe Zones:

These civilians live outside of safe zones either because they choose to do so or because they do not have a suitable safe zone nearby.

Hostile Civilians: Civilians who choose not to live in safe zones can include large populations of hostile civilians. These can fall under a number of categories:

- Independence movements.
    - Groups seeking to split from the United States.
- Revolutionaries.
    - Groups seeking to overthrow the government of the United States.
- Anarchists.
    - Groups who do not recognize the authority of any organization.

Platoons and squads must constantly hone their combat skills to close, engage and destroy these elements as required.

It is likely that combating these elements will be counter-insurgency in nature rather than conventional warfare. FM 3-24 Counterinsurgency, FM 3-24.2 Tactics in Counterinsurgency and FM 3-07 Stability Operations will provide guidance.

Neutral civilians: Neither hostile nor accepting of the United States government, these groups choose to live outside of safe zones but do not take hostile action against the government. Assistance will be provided to these groups as required and squads and platoons tasked to deal with these populations will strive to win their hearts and minds through help, honor and courtesy.

Friendly civilians: These civilians may live outside safe zones by choice or because there are no suitable safe zones nearby. They are friendly towards the government and the military. Care must be taken not to anger these populations.

Transition to End of Counter-Zombie Operations

As Zombie formations are decimated and more areas are made safe for normal life, Counter-Zombie Operations will slow down in pace. Eventually the President of the United States will call for the end of Counter-Zombie Operations.

Post-Zombie Combat Operations

Although a return to peacetime conditions is favorable, the realities of a post-Zombie emergency world are unclear. The United States Army may be engaged in assisting Counter-Zombie Operations elsewhere in the world, or may be engaged in counter-insurgency operations at home. The US Army soldier and the organization as a whole must be able to adapt to and overcome all challenges of a post-Zombie emergency world.

Battle Drills

These battle drills exist to enable the squad and platoon to execute Counter-Zombie Operations with minimal leader input.

Battle Drill 1: QRF Response to Isolated Zombie Outbreak.

Situation: A platoon has been tasked with a rapidly evolving situation in a lightly populated area where Zombies have been sighted and are attacking the local population.

Step 1. Equip and Mount Vehicles. The platoon (or squad) quickly mounts vehicles with equipment necessary to fight Zombies.

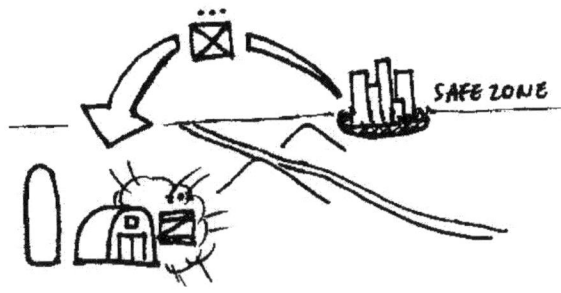

Fig 4.2 A platoon sized QRF takes advantage of rotary wing transport assets to quickly respond to a Zombie formation numbering about forty.

Step 2. Arrival at objective. Platoon or squad arrives at the objective, dismounts from vehicles and forms the arrow head formation and moves towards the direction of battle.

Fig 4.3 Arrow head formation.

Step 3. Engage Zombies. Platoon or squad engages Zombies and infected civilians.

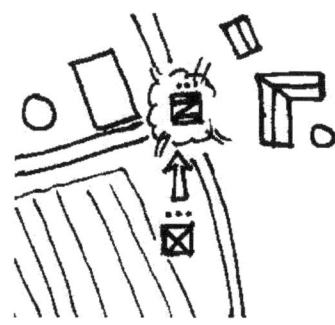

Fig 4.4 Platoon moves in and engages main Zombie formation.

Step 4. Final sweep. Platoon or squad goes room to room, inspecting civilians, looking for bitten civilians. Bitten civilians are escorted outside and dispatched in a secluded location.

Fig 4.5 The platoon splits up and clear buildings of Zombies and infected civilians.

Step 5. Final Cleanup. Platoon or squad calls in a chemical company to sanitize the area of the Zombie disease.

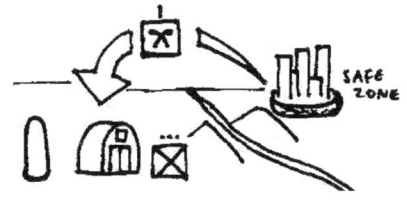

Fig 4.6 Chemical Company arrives.

Step 6. Return to base. Upon arrival of the chemical company, QRF passes on intelligence and information, mounts vehicles and returns to base.

Overview:

Step 1: Mount vehicles.

Step 2: Arrive at objective.

Step 3: Engage Zombies.

Step 4: Final sweep.

Step 5: Call chemical company.

Step 6: Return to base.

Battle Drill 2: Perimeter Defense against Heavy Zombie Onslaught.

Situation: A large Zombie formation arrives within 100-50m of the perimeter under the cover of darkness and fog. The message is relayed from the guard posts to the entire base/safe area.

Step 1. Equip and Move/Mount. The platoon receives notice of sudden and heavy Zombie presence outside the perimeter. Platoon equips and moves on foot if area under attack is under 200m or no vehicle is available. Otherwise, mount vehicles and move to area under attack.

Step 2. Line up on perimeter. The platoon lines up on perimeter. If the perimeter is secured by a chain link fence, soldiers will stick the grooves on their M-4/M-16 compensator in the chain link fence at a comfortable height. If the perimeter is secured by Hesco barriers, or other similar solid barriers (such as cargo containers), soldiers will climb to the top of it.

Step 3. Engage Zombies. Platoon opens fire and neutralizes the Zombie threat.

Overview:

Step 1: Move to perimeter.

Step 2: Line up on perimeter.

Step 3: Engage and neutralize Zombies.

FM 999-4

Appendix A

Keeping Current with Zombie Combat Command

Tactics, procedure, and doctrine regarding combating Zombies changes constantly and soldiers must stay up to date with the latest in Counter-Zombie Operations.

Staying up to date is easy. Subscribe to the Zombie Combat Command website and Facebook page.

Website: http://www.zombiecombatcommand.com

Facebook: http://www.facebook.com/pages/US-Army-Zombie-Combat-Command/156543711080815

If you have questions, comments or concerns, contact us at:

zombiecombatschool@gmail.com

Alternatively, you can send mail to:
    Zombie Combat Command
    10710 Gateway N Blvd #222
    El Paso, TX 79924

Appendix B

Additional Training Center at Fayetteville, Arkansas

Civilians and soldiers unable to attain a slot at the Zombie Combat School at Ft. Clement can get Zombie combat training and earn their Zombie qualification with Final DayZ. Contact Final DayZ on Facebook or through their website.

Website: http://survive.finaldayz.com/

Facebook: http://www.facebook.com/FinalDayZ

Point of contact is Instructor Mike Cunningham.

Final DayZ offers:

- Survival techniques and training
- Small unit combat tactics and training
- Zombie combat training`

Appendix C

Zombie Combat Command Online PX and Store

The Ft. Clement and Zombie Combat Command online PX and store are available for the purchase of gear approved by the Zombie Combat Command.

Online PX:
http://zombiecombatcommand.com/px/

Information on ordering Zombie skill tabs:
http://zombiecombatcommand.com/px/zombie-shoulder-tabs/

Zazzle Store (mugs, T-shirts etc.)
http://www.zazzle.com/army_zombie_combat/gifts

For any custom requests, email:
zombiecombatschool@gmail.com

Appendix D
Disclaimer

This publication is not published by, nor endorsed by the United States Army. We are not responsible for any injury, harm or mishaps that may occur as a result of following directions included within the text of this publication or elsewhere. Do not attempt anything without the proper training and/or supervision.
If you have any further questions, please send an email.

Also please note that FM 999-4 is not a free publication. Please do not distribute without the permission of the authors.

zombiecombatschool@gmail.com

Made in the USA
Lexington, KY
24 February 2018